The Flowering Word Tree

The Flowering Word Tree

Poems by

Ranjani Neriya

Cover by Shay Culligan
Cover art by Subir Biswas

ISBN: 978-1-63980-098-8

Kelsay Books
502 South 1040 East, A-119
American Fork, Utah 84003
Kelsaybooks.com

For my parents
Ramesh and Muktha Rao
who taught me to read and write

Acknowledgments

Grateful to the editors of the following publications where these poems first appeared, in slightly different versions.

In U.S.A.

Able muse: “Yarn”
Adanna literary journal: “Someone sings”
Beloit poetry journal: “Husk,” “Torque,” “Imagene,” “Workshop”
Many mountains moving: “Circadian”
Midwest poetry review: “Quarry”
Stonecoast review: “Chrysalis”
The listening eye: “The flowering word tree”
The macguffin: “Our god of mail,” “Cloth,” “Dimensions,” “Chapters”
Tule review: “Pilgrim”
The aurorean: “Space of shapes,” “Orbit,” “Bookmark”
Visions international journal: “The way to rapture”
WomenArts quarterly journal: “Ritual”
XCP(cross cultural poetics) journal: “Transparencies”

In India

Femina: “Wellspring”
Indian literature: “Those done days”
Midday: “Thirst”
Quest: “Lonely hour”
The Indian P.E.N: “Togetherness”
The illustrated weekly of India: “Lost ways”
The sunday standard: “Cat”

Contents

In the garden

Poems are imaginary gardens with real toads in them.
—Marianne Moore

i
be a creature of joy
in winged galoshes and
sap for syrup from tree to tree

ii
knock tentative knuckles
on a derelict house
till the scumbled rafters unlock a myth

iii
dip quill in a gentian blend, array
a covey of tanagers in flight
through sorrel sheaves of light

iv
listen to a plumage of airs
plucked from a tear-shaped lute
under a Galilean moon, arrive

v
at the pool of allophones, float
a petal-sloop with a two-leaved sail
and watch a real toad hop away.

Wellspring

somewhere between the lakes of paddy
and the rib-caged tawny tilt of trees
each tile-bruised morning limped in
to waken the blackened hearth to flame

six children opened like flowers
warmed to gruel, bore away to school
pickled-mango breath, to last
till the cow-dust trailed home

my mother was among them

to their father, tall-boned
in homespun zeal belonged
the teacher's wand that brought
mathematics and visionary worlds
to children of the cow-dust land,
just in case life needed in
blind corners of fate
a wick to glow from time to time

when I trod the lane
I could by no means verify where
mother had fed, hop-scotched
or readied a wellspring of calm for me
but I knew it was here that
angels grew wings
gentle as my mother's hands,
that she dwelt long
on this elysian drift

towing a kingfisher-bannered sky,
tooled my genes with poetry
somewhere between these lakes of paddy
and the rib-caged tawny tilt of trees.

Torque

of seasons awash with field-blue rain
some stilled to memory
a green-gold bamboo's
lean strokes on rushed gray,
tinkle of teacups in the air
silver lilt in mother's hair

in slithery rainwear
we shambled through
laterite spume alongside
the horse-drawn carriage
on steamy macadam,
satchels swilling with
covenanted fancies of
graven desks, smothered inkwells,
trooped a seven-furlong hour
to Miss Miranda's infinitude of verbs

we tapped boots on culverts
of sunken shale, swung on the
aerial braid of the banyan's
witching root, took time
to pop a barley-sugar twist
into the sleep-stuffed mouth
of the friendly tea-boy who,
palmyra parasol a-hoist,
ferried bronze-lathered brew
for the grocers' crew hefting
straw roundels rippled with rice,

the slow-falling structure of life
once in a while aborts
an attic pile, recalls
a torque, pure alluvial strain
the humming well of
a fretted bell-dream.

The flowering word tree

for R.

fan of eagles in a smolder of hills
homesteads tile-scrolled, sedgy streams
the banyan's bivouac
mango blossom thrum
sunny-voiced sonatina in
a teeming corridor of spice

to dream is to remember the forgotten

the word-tree, up-swung from
some dim niche of flowstone through
eon of slow root, slower petiole
monsoon's gouache granule
petal-thrall, fulgent and yellow-rayed

I remember

the earthen wishing bowl
the lantern of a long night
rapturous phoneme
wounds of life blazing
breath deep in the nectary
of the flowering word-tree

I dream

it is still half-light blotting
the night's wet silk
the remembered and the dream

it is too soon to forget.

Those done days

learning
just through percolation
under a woolpack sky
ablaze with prisms
after a monsoon shower

the foothills' dun leather
in a ferment, isinglass-y ponds
full of thirst,
lusty with knapweed and
mucilaginous dogbane

summers of new exercise books
forest tinctures inhaled
in the paring of pencils
with a razor blade,
clocking a pandemonium of
low-gravity ink bottles
pen-holders sharp as teeth,

the hum of conch-wells
the waterfront splashed
with silty tints of
the never-ever earth
chronicled, lambent
with citron pebble firth.

Husk

our trundle-tail Begum,
nosing into every leaf pile
alerted our mood
for woodnotes, far from
baying commerce, only treetops
churning a lapis sky,

romancing Shelley between
sips of thermos tea and
yeasty shags of bread, sour-sweet
from Lizzie Coutinho's bakery;

at the base of the brain there was
this delirious ticking
like the bruise of husk on
pearly sheaths of nascent dew
on the growing grass of our lives,

zest of hibiscus, screw-pine
silk-cotton splurge
a clear dream of water
no boulder big enough
to halt the rivering of
Periclean weather into
an Indian summer haze.

Catamaran tides

in the trudge of these wheeling needs
comes this gentle roll-back
of star-clocks, silence of chimes,
a foothold of a tired trek, a rest-house
a shot-silver beach, slow-borne
as the groundsel's yellow-rayed bloom

when

a frothy veil slid over the
sun's uncertain face,
teal feet shackled vermeil riffs
in the casuarina's tracery,
lanterns stuttered to flame
luster of lute roused
our minds to a stillness and
afar, in the thatched huts
smoky-eyed fisher-folk rose to song
by their feeble hearths

memory, like sand-script on rock-face
the whispery oracle of the sea
so long in its tale-telling
this life of abstractions, worlds
known ventured unlearned,
of tides like destiny, dissolved
severally to an aloneness of air
a wandered away shore.

The women of Bethany

to the chapel of Bethany, archaic, orieled
beyond the school-yard's tartan territory
came the women, in a rustle of saris
seersucker gowns, sandaled feet
hymn books in hand, wafting
a churn of coconut and spice;

their chant-like *Konkani* colloquy
had wisdom they meant to give, perhaps
a force-electric of engaging pain
but unhurt, young, I was listening elsewhere
like a dervish caught in a singing swirl
of the casuarina's horsetail-rain,
a cumulonimbus cloud, somewhere
purpling a creeper of honeyed bells

ringing in the silence of distant lanes
which I could not make them hear,
the tumult of an alphabet just begun
hard by that chapel of Bethany.

Lost ways

when the hay-cart left
we streamed up the ladder
fell as dizzy shadows along chinks
that goldened the wooden walls
of the loft where the bales
threw a siege of brisk light
for the freedom of our souls

from there to watch
the tinsmith in the yard below
pave old copper with moonbeams
gray beard singing in that noon
wreathed with young skies
blowing soft through the trees
where our laughter rang
perhaps for the last time
trilled to country land home
a way of life that grew
wise and beautiful with the elements.

Thirst

the woman waits

her chipped bowl
gathers thirst

she will presently
swill her parched eyes
with a tucked-away
remnant of life,

a still from some
dust borne caravan
where water was sweet

because sorrow must not kill
nor feet begin to sleep

on unending road
morrow is mesmeric
unfailingly there,
sometimes with hope
of strange deliverance

she must do what she has to do
burn her body on
one matchstick every day.

Quarry

in riddling light
when shade-shackled space
dissolves in frets of brick-gold
the mind lifts
an ancient timeframe,
an earth hollow on
a zinc edge of sound
where rawboned men
retextured endlessly
hot rims of laterite,
stone-burdened women
washed up in the
freshet eyes of children
their sweat of hope

I wonder if they ever found
somewhere
balsam of monsoonal cloud
for quarried hands,
a hammock of winding sleep,
whether they walked away
from hearthstone grief
to a breath of lilies
on undented pond,
picked kayak freedom
in glideaway dreams.

Cat

she comes to lap
drippings from uncleansed pots
the color of newly turned earth;
I go out to meet her
but she is ever staid, parsimonious
our bond is unequated genetics,
a creature respect of
our separate caprice

to keep her a moment
preened in my sight
as she knuckles sleek
onto her last lap of wall,
I hold her eyes with mine
dredging their strange hurt passion
for relevance;

she uncoils
pulsations from her throat,
teeth plectrum strumming
a tremolo, and that is as far
as she deigns to reach,

then in a blur-electric
of impeccable faience
she is gone.

Circadian

warrens of space
lignin-dissolution
unheard sound-shape

flute among reeds
daughter-heart revisiting
earth mother's home

the ocelot-drowse
glue glint off
a minivet's nest

bee buzz alliteration
of the pollen tale,
nucleate fieldwork

shiva-dance of universe
a dervish in song-whirl
a *kecan* in prayer glade

circadian travelogue
the breathing ash-pile and
seed's recollection of growth.

Lonely hour

I cannot say who planted
those shadows in the sun
whence tempest-wild upon the fine
torrid gaze of summer day
this sullen fist, silent mist
tossing up a starry spray

those dark hooves of bodiless air
seem to crate suddenly
from that razor-sleek sparrow-way
where sea and sky are one

there is grief in twilight's undoing
grief of an ignorant tale
of loneliness that may never end
and tomorrow always far away.

Someone sings

rose-bud and hawk-view
silk pewter ink
is the bodyless-ness of sleep
whence sun wakens
and in my mind someone sings
soft as lamb fleece

a bent woman in a purple cape
taps her cane, past
cloud pebble stream
keeps time to someone singing
in my mind an old pastoral ditty
as she walks by the potter's wheel
where a knob of clay
pirouettes to shape
to the tune of someone
singing in my mind;

I distil birdsong
into a cup and drink,
follow the bent woman
as far as the potter's wheel
and we sit on a ledge amid
a slowness in the girth of trees
the bent woman and I,
hard by the pirouetting urn
on the potter's wheel
and we listen companionably
to someone singing in my mind
that longago pastoral ditty.

Chrysalis

it was the mineral mint of terrain
which accomplished much more
for the hum in the chrysalis
to engage belief,
carillon of the pristine
what chimed us into vortices

an epic event of sky-craft
a river gong hollowing a cave
minarets of moonbeams
rain trees brindled with damsel flies
blowing magic into our god-gazing minds,
in a dark core to find unstruck light,

when the best part of sleep was wakening.

Our god of mail

long before e-mail it was paper mail
long before texting it was penfriending

the only god we worshipped
was Postman Thimma
of the thousand-rupee smile,
a timeworn 'Gandhi cap'
aslant on a mop of tawny hair

when his bicycle belled on macadam
we flew out of our homes like banners

under the guava tree's canopy
on a carpet of traceries, palmettes
we read each-others' letters
exchanged dreams and albums
mounted photos with paper corners

no handshakes, no spoken words, sheer exotica
like red beryls in the green spin of the mango leaf,
geography of the unseen a tap on our window
a fabled footfall in the laterite lilt of our lane.

Transparencies

some sorties are just
leaf and rumble
a ceaseless universe
that does not allow sleep

the axle's needle wail
on puckered macadam
means an oxen team is
burdened with pain

some clouds do not rain
merely skim darkling waves
while the beached shell's sandy mouth
fills with sky

a candle must burn somewhere
at both ends to
demonize a god, cause
sudden midnight at noon

transparencies
redefining perspective
in this cerebral chink between
darkness ahead, darkness behind.

The way to rapture

the way to rapture
is sinuous and deep
a saw through water
a vanishing crease

a hunch of photons
in a starlit pool
mind's locked tune
searching for keys

you must listen
to the buzz in the body
deaf as sleep,
the syllabary of bees

dip into a trove of color
which flowers excavate
in the velvet chalice's
dulcet inlay; meanwhile

lapwings in the bushes
may have seized the clue
as they chatter up noisily
the succulence of shoots

that the way to rapture
landborne or mountain hoar
is just another way to fly
an attentiveness of being.

Yarn

I feel her lithe fingers piano-keying
the lovely spun yarn of my sleeve
and I deliberate

who can say what seized her day
did starlings glow gamboge in the hayrick
a frog gloss his amber gaze
to compliment a ladybug ambling away

who can tell if she was
a wispy five foot one
her glasses almost chin deep
her topknot a swiveled gray
and she, weaving
her wood-smoky life
of *roti* and tea with a smile

or was an unhurried child
still looking out of her eyes
minting small awakenings in a
niche of mind, and
who can say whether
a fantasia made landfall
at her feet, her body
a loosened harp
trilling an odyssey
on a kayak to her very own
lake-island of being,
so the piano-keying fingers on my sleeve.

Cloth

worsted, it was mostly colonial
immured in a shackled weave
home-wheeled, it became
Gandhi's dream
a handmade revolution

the fragments of holy minds
sky-knit with the skein of trees
is a denim-lapis archive
calico-d in dips of gold
a snow-swept revelation

it is how cloth is spent
to threadbare the lived-in field
esoteric netting which spills loose
the broken fruit of flesh, cloth

as fabrication of unknown seam.

Imagene

Da Vinci's notes, meticulously scripted
left-handed and backward
were construed only through a mirror

imagene. curvilinear, unequally pulled
replenished, concerted on illusion
that the hidden is safe

so is the unreadable instant
till we stand in another's eye
to see ourselves, wait

for the silvery thistles on still water
to release our shape
pluck our voice from the wind

the unreflected, what steadies
the fulcrum, imminent with
revelation, abides to make

the code manifest, linking
all the while sun-soar to
sea-floor to cave-mouth
holds each one in its spell

the ashen flake
the clear green air.

Dimensions

I am more river than
the gushing rosebay
silted up in the
slowly falling wall

more pond than
the mushroom swirling
in the cast iron skillet
over flaming coal

I am more lake than
the blind eye sailing
fringe of coast
on unmapped days

more sea than
a rainy wafer of sun
stuck in the roaring
throat of night

I am more stream than
wavering droplet on a glass
so ice-friendly and
and green with stars

I am huge torrent, thwarted
by scorpion-whips of light
by the enigma of dark
the filigree of a sand grain.

Ritual

you touch the bench
then the tree
it changes the way you breathe

you toss a stone
endanger the breeze
23 crows or thereabout, flee

the *tulsi* on the windowsill
is diminished by grace
its prayer, a roar in the throat

you take a knife to a melon
humming hefty with summer
boats of red ice unkeel

the dog barks at a paper plane
piloted from a tall cornice
it has sky as its passenger

from room to room
in search of thought, learn
that one peg holds all.

Chapters

the morning reads
a green apple mint into
the coffee's whipped brown pour
silver rune of spoon and bowl,

onto the less ordinary
the squirrel's coal-bright gaze
geese-clarion overhead
earth tones, the elemental
dipping, vanishing page

elsewhere, shrapnel inurns hearths
children die in a schoolroom blaze,
such hole-in-the-heart moments
their stay long and tidal

night; and the freshly rosined ripple
of a violin's bow, as if pining
for a lost wellhead, wilts the air
where I sit by a single leaf of light
to read again this terrible absence
of your face near mine.

Bookmark

I dislike dog-earing the page
of a book or putting it face down
like a picketed pyramid

it deserves a mark of grace

I respect the book's aspiration
of reading life into
someone's thought
perhaps, jack-hammered or
whittled through long nights,

pages redolent with
the welkin's hum, above
a conference of trees,
a vignette thronged
with the etch of ink
a ratchet of machinery

all trimmed and jacketed
to arrive like a long-lost love
to seat me in an easy-chair
to a camaraderie of words,
life's slackening trail
salvaged by a book's mark.

Space of shapes

form is fugitive

it is not of the wheel
carving the shade

nor of the vane
flying the wind

but an eagle-spun sky
omniscient and blue;

form is fugitive
continuity is life, so

dislodge the pearly marble
from the block-hole, seep into

all shades of sorrel and
wallflower and mashed grape.

ponder the deer's seeking
hoofed in last night's rain

the latchet of fern
the perimeter of stone

continuity is the mythic gondola
wise to the shifting resonance of seas.

Ageing

you climb a difficult mountain called sleep
and prepare to tackle day-rise rife with oddities,
the biotic beaten to a thready rummage and
the personal god a moonshined lazuli,

with the mind's accessory in a settled passive
the blunt surround seems to drift away, but
there is this tingling, like a steered stint for a
filial wage paid in some stone-writ dictate

so, with a huff and a creak, an elderly chair arrays
a faithful view by the window, a gathering of tools
patter on water, cheeps in tansy, pen on paper
the skirl of a new notion in the breeze,

and those unforgotten maidenhair lanes open
say, it isn't done yet.

Workshop

slacken those jute-strung almanacs
blow-dust those shellacked urns
finger the flaky diluvium
of fragrant panniers
tread tenderly, it is a churn
of Minton, molten with star-fall
and tinted thimblefuls from
a bedewed belvedere

how brokenly it gathers
whole, this whispery coda
annealed in a fire of anecdote
of kenaf tethered, roof
osier-d, ashlar river-whorled
blue-plink of adze, chintzy
all smoothened to life's music

how we slapped linen
at the rill, how we fired
a stone of joy
stoned a fire of grief,
it's all about longings
as they say, be a drop
in the ocean to find
the ocean in a drop

the varied aggregate, mind-body
electrum, thirstful of the
damson trail, resinous fume
breath alight with ballade
fill the mazer, tipple and flow
in the crook of heart to know,
one leaf it is mints the whole green glade
one nimbus wheels this cosmic clay.

Pilgrim

a window is a place in time
through which the world
gets darker

the face with no sorrow is rare
so is the land with no name

speculum of cinder wakens
a rush of speech in the head
that the fire is out and it is
about time to shake out
the scarf, bag the spares

bondage is sheer wearied unwise

before the light steals in and
ignites a honeysuckle lane
sparrows elate and that hollow
scooped by a longago sadness
wears a face,

it feels bound to hustle the cane
be gone and away.

Togetherness

is the simple extrusion
of beginning to live
beyond the winds of change
I in this room,
a scaling graph dizzying
the permanent perimeter
of brainstorms,
with a pen to pile
dwindling segments of heat
back into bones.

life has still
one more voltage to go
I have this land
a tree to plant
a pot to scour
a bolt of sun unhewn
in the attic store,
I have this togetherness
a pain of touch
gathering everywhere,
bringing word
that life is lonely
and I belong nowhere.

This sheath, this beingness

for S.

it does not ravel the whole code
this reticulation of mutant dust
rustled amber of a neural cell

this intaglio of feet in sand
stippled gold of lake shot with
tan of seed and weed and the
valorous stance of a lone fallen leaf

this pan of fungus, having seized
tremor of mineral, buzz of pollen
hovers in a scattershot
of dandelion lisle;

in this rhythm of being
is a feather chant of aloneness
an eddying branch gauging a stream
a bees-way hush into nectary

this solander of atoms, calendar of stone
where water first tasted green
is the cortex, mathematics of life
nomadic, ever pitching sheer tepees of light.

To the 6-million-year-old footprints

the footprints were discovered in Laetoli, Tanzania, by Mary Leakey

don't go any further
now that we have found you
rest awhile

flag us off gently
through daggled dykes of mist
teach us

the steep terror of ice-hills
jungles of roaring dark
of adze, flint, gourd

germinant spore, husky grain
berry-blur and elk-tide and
such other countless gold

a lost loess, the language
you wandered in, the deep
bleed of your healing;

so to hosanna, earth-chant
as we invest
our footprint in yours

and marvel
how sync-d the shape
how celestial the clay.

Wonderstruck

wonder is private

the rolling stone rips
the pond's breathy calm
to feel its own

hasten to the aid of the
bursting chrysalis and
the swallow-tail butterfly dies

wonder is innate

a spirit trail hums in the
random, uneven spread
of wind-burst and star-lure

random as mind, meandering
to be within sight of an
edged-on-wonder universe

wonder is peregrine

what fluke, seraphic, nebulous
moved in that long ago tinting
of tesserae in the dawn of distance

to unzip helix streams onto our
wonderstruck millenniums,
forever awake.

Orbit

dark finger, write in loops of gold
on mirror shards of evening when
its color of rice husk turns
the color of aniseed, and
all distance comes back
in search of the lamp we lit
by the russet seat near the lotus pond

I am the wanderer clothed in the
skin of stars, forever returning
to the island of my father,
antigonon's coral wreath, to the
belled veil and floral seam,
anklets silvering in logfires
and strains of sitar

stay with me, let us heal the
smear in the bulbul's throat
the bloodied power of its wing

fingertips they say, keep alive
the spirit wind of our lineage,
wait till I finish my song.

About the Author

Born and educated in the coastal town of Mangalore, S. India, Ranjani Neriya lived in Mumbai (Bombay) with her family for many years before moving to the U.S. She resides in Michigan.

www.ingramcontent.com/pod-product-compliance
Lightning Source LLC
LaVergne TN
LVHW051021080826
845145LV00009B/2743

* 9 7 8 1 6 3 9 8 0 0 9 8 8 *